Get Set, GO!

Written by Sasha Morton

Get set.

Kick it in the net!

Get in the mud.

Tuck it in and run!

Go on the top and tuck in.

Dip in!

Sit in it and get set.

Go in the pit.

Pick it up.

Tip it in!

Get in a gap and run!

Got it!

Get set to go

kick

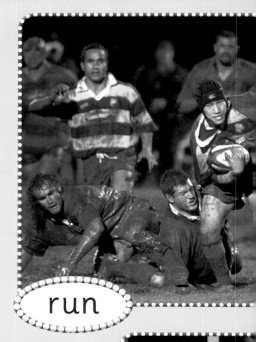

run

get set

14

tip

dip

run

15

Ideas for reading

Written by Clare Dowdall, PhD
Lecturer and Primary Literacy Consultant

Learning objectives: *(reading objectives correspond with Pink B band; all other objectives correspond with White band)* read simple words by sounding out and blending the phonemes all through the word from left to right; read a range of familiar and common words and simple sentences independently; explain organisational features of texts, including alphabetical order, layout, diagrams, captions, hyperlinks and bullet points; explain ideas and processes using imaginative and adventurous vocabulary and non-verbal gestures to support communication

Curriculum links: P.E.

Focus phonemes: s, a, t, p, i, n, m, d, g, o, ck, e, u, r, k

Fast words: to, go, the

Resources: whiteboards, magnetic letters, fast word cards, ICT

Word count: 50

Getting started

- Practise reading the fast words using word cards. Remind children about tricky parts of the words, e.g. they do not have normal short vowel sounds.

- Read the title together. Ask children to suggest what *Get Set* means and when they have heard it. Discuss why the word *Go!* has an exclamation mark, and how it should be read.

- Look at the picture on the front cover. Ask children to describe what they can see and to name the equipment being used, e.g. sprinting, racing trainers, starting blocks. Support children to use adventurous vocabulary.

Reading and responding

- Turn to pp2–3. Model how to read the text, sounding out and blending new words, e.g. *k-i-ck*, and then to reread the whole sentence for fluency. Remind children that *ck* is a digraph that makes one sound.

- Look at p4 together. Ask children to read the text and discuss what game is being played.

- Ask children to read to p13 independently, identifying what sport is being played on each new page. Remind them to blend sounds to read new words, and to reread whole sentences to develop fluency.